NOT IN SERVICE

The Afterlives of Classic British Buses

DOUGLAS G. MacDONALD

The History Press

Until the end of the 'swinging sixties', and in some cases into the early part of the following decade, no fairground was complete without an old bus or two. Most were used for living accommodation, some for carrying equipment and/or generating power. CHT 334 was a Bristol JNW new to Bristol Tramways in 1936. Rebodied by ECW to B35R in 1949, the bus was withdrawn at the age of twenty-three. Bought by Southampton-based showman Davis, the vehicle passed to Bates of Putney in 1964, in whose ownership it is pictured here. The single-decker was last sighted in the summer of 1970. (Author's Collection)

First published 2009

The History Press
The Mill, Brimscombe Port
Stroud, Gloucestershire, GL5 2QG
www.thehistorypress.co.uk

British Library Cataloguing in Publication Data.
A catalogue record for this book is available from the British Library.

ISBN 978 0 7524 5083 4

Typesetting and origination by The History Press
Printed in Great Britain

CONTENTS

Acknowledgements   4

Introduction   5

1   Builders' and Contractors' Buses   6

2   Cafés, Catering and Mobile Shops   17

3   Transport(er)s of Delight!   31

4   Exhibitionists   37

5   Community Service   45

6   Caravans and Living Accommodation   55

7   Play Days   65

8   Dancers on 'Deckers ... and Mobile Musicians   71

9   Religion on the Road   79

10   Fruit-Picking Passengers   87

11   Extended Service   91

12   People Carriers   99

13   Overseas Omnibuses   107

14   Fairs' Stage   115

ACKNOWLEDGEMENTS

To produce and compile a book on such a specialised and yet wide-ranging transport topic, I have had to enlist and call upon the help of many people, organisations and resources. I record my sincere thanks in the list below to all of them for their willing contributions, be it photographs, information or knowledge.

A special debt of gratitude is recorded to Mike Street and Donald Hudson for their generosity in voluntarily offering up a large supply of topical images, accompanied by their relevant details. I am also grateful for the significant efforts of Dick Gilbert in identifying several 'unknown' vehicles, courtesy of his own knowledge and his excellent 'Classic Buses' website.

My own photographic collection has been amassed over almost four decades, and in using images from this large stockpile it has been impossible to identify all sources and originators; if anyone has been inadvertently overlooked I duly apologise.

Peter Findlay; Mike and Pat Sutcliffe – The Leyland Society; Chris Knight – Bristol Vehicles Bus Group; Ian Findlay/Phil Logie – North East Bus Preservation Trust; Nigel Mason – Thamesdown Transport; Malcolm Asquith – Crossley Motors Group; Neil Gow – AEC Society; Tim Moss – Leyland National Group; Mike Thomas – Scammel Register Group; Rob Sly – Bristol Commercial Vehicles website; John Wakefield – TheWakefield Files; Peter Gould Fleetlists; Bus Lists on the Web; PSV Circle; The Omnibus Society; Charles Drew – Amber Foundation; Keith Beeden – Sheffield Bus Museum; James Darrington – Music Links; Kenny Barclay; Donald Stirling; Royal Zoological Society of Scotland; Pat Lee – The Jesus Army; A.E. Jones; the Revd Patrick Coleman; Gordon Stirling; David J. Hancock; Allan T. Condie; Dale Tringham; Derek Jones; Stephen Dowle; Paul Pearson – Potteries Omnibus Preservation Society; 'Traveller Dave'; David Longbottom; Dave Carter – BriSCA.

INTRODUCTION

From the early days of the motor bus, to the streamlined versions of the twenty-first century, passenger-carrying public service vehicles have been a familiar sight in Britain. Many buses were simply scrapped or broken-up when withdrawn after a lengthy service with original operators, while others may have been sold on to new owners at an earlier age for further PSV usage. However, the lives of many more were prolonged by being deployed on a variety of duties and purpose by a wide spectrum of buyers, who adapted vehicles to suit their own specialised needs.

From fairgrounds to food, from builders' transport to berry buses, this book looks at most of the varied uses in which second-hand buses/coaches have been engaged, from the 1950s to the more recent future. I have endeavoured to cast the net as wide as possible in terms of the content. While Scottish vehicles had their own detailed focus in a previous volume (*Saved from the Scrapyard – Scottish Buses Recycled*, Tempus 2006), it would be narrow-minded not to include images from north-of-the-border in this publication, none of which appeared in the earlier book. Similarly, I have made a conscious effort not to overload the following pages with former London Transport buses, purely because of the numbers of their fleet becoming non-PSVs etc., and surely deserving more in-depth coverage, and certainly by someone who can specialise in this particular field.

Please note that while endeavouring to trace the history or origins of every vehicle featured, with as much information as possible, even with the wonderful World Wide Web, this proved to be difficult, or nigh-impossible in a few cases.

I hope the range of photographs appeals not only to bus/transport enthusiasts, but also to 'nostalgia lovers' of bygone decades.

1

BUILDERS' AND CONTRACTORS' BUSES

Following the dark days of the Second World War, the United Kingdom saw a building boom from the 1950s. War-damaged housing stock had to be replaced, and inner-city slums and old property were being phased out to make way for new, modern homes in most local authority areas, with many towns and cities expanding beyond their original boundaries. The implementation of designated 'new towns', the growing demand for private housing, and new-build factories and industrial developments meant the entire construction industry never had it so good. The one potential drawback was a logistical problem. Remember, this was an age when car ownership was in the minority, and the working class in particular relied on public transport for work and pleasure purposes. Even with a far better provision of bus services than in evidence today, it could be difficult for tradesmen and labourers alike to reach out-of-town sites for early morning starts five or six days a week.

A sensible solution was found by most of the major, and many of the smaller, construction companies by laying on dedicated private transport for their workforce. This led to the purchase of withdrawn buses and coaches either direct from the operators, or via dealers. Some companies repainted these vehicles in their own 'livery', while others simply deleted legal lettering and fleetnames, and ran them in the well-known colours of their original or subsequent owners. As a boy growing up in Central Scotland, I used to explore building sites hoping to catch a glimpse of an old bus, especially from the Alexander or Central SMT fleets, while my chums were more concerned with sourcing empty lemonade bottles for the 3d returnable deposit!

New to Hebble in 1946, this AEC Regal II had a thirty-five-seat body by Weymann. After withdrawal, it passed to John Morgan (Builders) Ltd. (Author's Collection)

This Dennis Lancet K3 double-decker was just one of forty similar vehicles delivered new to Aldershot & District Traction Co. between 1948 and 1952. GAA 628 still carries the green/cream colours of A&D but is now in the ownership of local builder H. Crudgington. (Author's Collection)

Laing was just one of the 'national' housebuilders who accrued a sizeable fleet of vehicles to ferry their employees to developments up and down the country. *Above*: New to Ribble Motor Services, FFR 355 was an all-Leyland Royal Riger from 1950. (Donald Hudson) *Below*: KRR 844 looks extremely clean to be running in and out of building sites! The Leyland PD2 may have been just acquired by Laings from East Midlands. (Author's Collection)

Thetford Construction acquired this Bristol/ECW single-decker when it was fifteen years old. The vehicle had been new in 1956 to Eastern Counties as their LC/511, and was actually converted to one-man-operation (OMO) just a year after delivery. (Author's Collection)

LNF 553 carries distinctive Burlingham coachwork. The 1949 Leyland PS2/1 had been new to Mason of Manchester before being bought by E.H. Roberts Plant. This photo was snapped at Southend in 1965. (Author's Collection)

Yuill be surprised to learn that these two buses had different owners! *Above*: Cecil M. Yuill was a Hartlepool-based building firm whose main projects were on Tyneside and Teesside, although occasionally further afield. All-over white with company name and 'cubic' logo was the standard colour scheme. Former West Yorkshire OWX 135 was a Bristol LS6G of 1955 with C39F bodywork by ECW. (Donald Hudson) *Below*: EO 8652 was one of a ten-strong batch of Crossley DD42s delivered new to Barrow Corporation in May 1948. The 8ft-wide double-decker later passed to J. Yuill in the Glasgow area, and had company north of the border, as a few of her 'sisters' were snapped up by Clyde Coast Services and other independent operators. (Author's Collection)

A true North West of England vehicle. Built by Leyland in 1953, this Royal Tiger was new to North Western Road Car Co. and, after withdrawal eight years later, sold to Leonard Fairclough, no relation to the (fictitious) builder of the time who was a regular for many years in *Coronation Street*! The picture dates from February 1965, and was taken in the environs of Manchester. (Author's Collection)

Picking up workers in Durham, this 1950 AEC Regent III had been DR 573 in the fleet. (Author's Collection)

In 1880, George Wimpey established a stone-working business in Hammersmith, West London. The company's reputation grew rapidly; they were responsible for major building and tramway projects, and as early as the 1920s started house-building. Now an international business, the name lives on today as the Taylor-Wimpey Group. *Above*: With 'regional' bases, the company had surely the largest fleet of buses and coaches to transport their sizeable workforce. Most of the vehicles came from Southdown, like this 1954 Leyland Tiger Cub with Beadle C41C bodywork. George Wimpey actually acquired more than half of this seventy-five-strong batch after withdrawal by Southdown. (Author's Collection) *Below*: All of the vehicles purchased were painted in the company colours of yellow and black, with the name in large bold lettering. With Harrington Cavalier body, 2702CD was a Leyland Leopard L2T delivered in 1961, and these stylish coaches were probably Southdown's best-known coaches of their generation. (Author's Collection)

Trent Motor Services was the original operator of this AEC Regal I from 1947. At the age of eleven, the bus received a makeover, being converted by original bodybuilder Willowbrook from B35F to FDP39F, in which condition it was acquired by Wimpey some four years later. (Author's Collection)

George Wimpey also bought second-hand stock 'oop North'. With a fifty-three-seat lowbridge Brush body, ACK 135 was new to Ribble in 1940. Withdrawn in 1952, Wimpey used the double-decker for four years before selling it to Salford dealer Frank Cowley. The Leyland TD7 bussed more builders between 1958 and 1960 with Finland of Manchester before it finally fell victim to Cowley's blowtorch! (Author's Collection)

Famous independent Delaine of Bourne added this stylish Leyland with Duple Ambassador body to their fleet in 1952. Sold just seven years later to Johnson of Rushden, the coach was then added to the 'workies' ranks operated by national contractor Taylor Woodrow, no doubt providing a very comfortable ride for their workforce. (Author's Collection)

Seddon Atkinson were better known for building lorries, but they made a late entry into the PSV market by developing an underfloor-engined single-decker. Venture of Consett, Co. Durham bought six Atkinson Alphas, some of which later passed to North East house-builder Leech. All of their buses bore the legend 'Buy a Leech Home' in a large script style. RPT 131 was No.171 in the Venture fleet, new in 1955 and withdrawn twelve years later. (R.F. Mack)

Bristol's short-bodied, front-entrance Lodekka, the FSF, found little popularity in the nationalised Scottish Bus Group. Only Central SMT bought the marque as new vehicles. From 1962 DGM 439 was Central's B139, and almost two decades after entering service is captured with George Wilson. The Stonehouse company had a varied fleet over the years, but ex-Central buses were always evident in the Lanarkshire yard. (Author's Collection)

A Guy Arab III from 1952 with Roe B41C bodywork, PHN 706 was originally Darlington Corporation No.33 (number still carried). It is shown here working for Dixon & Nice in Stockton-on-Tees in December 1970 but clearly in need of a good wash! (Donald Hudson)

Harry Cruden started his company in the 1940s in Musselburgh to replace war-damaged housing stock in the Edinburgh area. As the company grew in the following two decades, they undertook building projects in other parts of the country. Perhaps not surprisingly, when Crudens implemented the use of staff transport, they turned to the 'cast-offs' of SMT/Scottish Omnibuses, with most transactions done via capital dealer James Locke. New in 1937 with Cowieson body, this AEC Regal II was B166 in the SMT Ranks, and was rebodied by Alexander in 1947, as pictured here. (Author's Collection)

This chapter concludes with something of a mystery vehicle! Registration mark 'CU' was allocated to South Shields. One theory is that this is a Leyland PS half-cab coach which has been rebodied, possibly by Beadle. The photograph was taken in April 1965, and it is believed Firth was a Yorkshire construction firm. (Author's Collection)

2

CAFÉS, CATERING AND MOBILE SHOPS

In the jargon-overloaded new millennium, the term 'MPV' is readily recognised and well-used in the upper echelons of the car sales market. However, it would be equally fair to suggest that the humble bus was actually the real Multi-Purpose Vehicle in the course of its lifetime, as this book (hopefully) illustrates! People carriers, service vehicles, living accommodation and many other adapted uses could be added to the vehicle log-book.

This chapter looks at buses which no longer carry people, but which serves them up food, drink and hospitality. With today's extensive motorway network, there exists a plethora of 'Services', but for years on the highways and byways a thirst would be quenched and hunger pangs quelled by stopping to sample the culinary delights of a roadside/layby café or snack-bar. Indeed, even today they survive on many trunk and other routes, but very few serveries started life as a PCV, to use the modern tag ... purpose-built trailers, old vans, ambulances and even the occasional caravan are the norm.

In the 1950s and '60s when the majority of married women were 'housewives' and in an era prior to the 'stock-up for a fortnight/month at the twenty-four-hour supermarket' culture, mobile shops provided a welcome service to suburban estates and housing schemes all across the country. From my own pre-school days, I recall a variety of wheeled purveyors on a daily basis – bakers, butchers, fishmongers, grocers, not forgetting the vans from respective departments of the local Co-Operative. One of my late father's friends went into the fruit and veg business, and from the outset he bought old buses – Bedford OB coaches, ex-local authority Bedford SBs (only one at a time!) and a few others. Sadly, no photographic evidence of any of these vehicles was ever taken.

Corporate Hospitality has become big business, and for many companies a necessary ingredient in the commercial calendar. For outdoor events like Race Meetings, Country/Trade Shows etc., some firms converted buses into mobile eateries and entertainment centres.There have also been a number of catering companies who specialise in serving the needs and appetites of the film and television industry on location, or at live outside broadcasts.

On the following pages, the images will show that all of these roles have been undertaken by second-hand, or even older, buses and coaches.

R.C. Saunders was still 'frying tonight' in 2005 at Enfield from this Bedford SB with 'butterfly'-shaped radiator grille. (Richard Haughey)

Opposite above: New to Liverpool Corporation (and then Merseyside PTE), RKA 955G was just one of 110 Leyland Panthers bought by the municipal operator. After withdrawal, the MCW-bodied (B47D) bus went to Hulleys of Bastow for further stage service. Thereafter, for almost twenty-five years, it could be found as a café on the A6 in Ambergate, between Matlock and Derby. In February 2008, the emerald green vehicle was bought by Merseyside Transport Trust, and it is thought has been used as a source of valuable spares for another ex-Liverpool Panther under their restoration (FKF 933G). (Author's Collection)

Opposite below: This Bristol FLF is pictured back at its old 'home' in September 1983, at Trent's Derby Depot Open Day. It was new to Midland General as No.309 before joining the Trent MS ranks as 748. Pennine Pizza of Huddersfield bought and converted it in 1999. (Author's Collection)

With contemporary Alexander body, KDW 83F was part of an octet of Leyland Atlanteans bought new by Newport Corporation in 1968. Fitted with a newer-style front lower panel during service in Wales, the double-decker became 'The Burger Dream'. No doubt a favourite on the menu was a DOUBLE Cheeseburger! (Mike Street)

Opposite above: JTU 588T was new to Crossville Wales in 1978 (SNG 588). After withdrawal it was deployed for many years as a roadside café, before being rescued for preservation. The Leyland National has now been restored in NBC livery, and is resident at the Scottish Vintage Bus Museum in Fife. (Author's Collection)

Opposite below: This small Seddon Pennine was new to Edinburgh Corporation in 1973. Along with sister 109, they passed to Stoniers/Berresfords in Staffordshire at the time of the miners' strikes in the 1980s, and actually arrived with their windows 'caged over'. With 'PAYE' sign still in place, 108 became a snack bar in the Barnsley area. (Martyn Hearson)

No seaside visit was complete without enjoying an ice cream! This vending vehicle has a real tale to tell. The twenty-seat Guy Wolf was new in 1935 to Llandudno Urban District Council (UDC). It was fitted with removable/foldable side panels for use as an open-sided bus. After withdrawal in 1960, the Guy stayed on the coast, and possibly in Llandudno itself, and served as an ice cream van. After many years of supplying 99s and sliders to day-trippers and holidaymakers, the not-so-big-bad Wolf was bought for preservation, lovingly restored to LUDC colours, and is still extant. (Author's Collection)

Obvious signs apart, this Daimler still resembles a coach, but is sadly deceptive. Despite the contemporary hype by the manufacturer, the Roadliner never really took the British bus market by storm, and many operators who bought them moved the vehicles on fairly swiftly, due to expensive running costs and poor performance. MDH 212E started life with Central Coaches of Walsall, but ended up as a café on the fringes of Nuneaton bus station. (Author's Collection)

A 1978 Leyland version of the Fleetline, with seventy-five-seat NCME bodywork, this
double-decker was new to Greater Manchester PTE as their 8006. Later working for
Thamesdown Transport in Swindon, the bus travelled across the country as late as 2001
to Bluebird Travel in Norfolk, before becoming a mobile café in the same county. (Author's
Collection)

The oldest vehicle in this chapter started life in 1928 as MS 8270, an Albion PK26, with
Alexander body and new to H. Pender of Falkirk. W. Alexander's bus operations took over
the independent in 1931 when the vehicle became initially 688 and then C87 in the famous
'Bluebird' fleet. Withdrawn in 1934, the thirty-seater was sold eighteen months later via
Millburn Motors the Glasgow dealer to an unknown owner in Inverness. The Albion is caught
on camera in the Highland capital, in its role as a static café/canteen. (Author's Collection)

Above and below: This East Lancs-bodied Leyland Leopard was new in February 1971 to Eastbourne Corporation. It is seen here in ultimate use as 'Butler's Café'. The view below shows the double-door arrangement, while in service with Eastbourne. (Author's Collection/below Roger King)

Still wearing the colours of the original owner, this ex-Bristol Omnibus 'L' type is on the road as a mobile shop selling fruit and veg in the Barnsley area. The price of strawberries was only *2s 6d* per lb in this 1960s shot! When new in 1942, it carried a Bristol Utility UB33F body and was No.2167 in the Bristol Tramways & Carriage Co. The vehicle was refitted in 1955 with the B35R body from BT&C's DHY 654. After its body makeover, the bus remained in service for a further six years. (R.F. Mack)

From the seashores of the South Coast to the mill towns of the North West – that was the later-life change for this once-handsome Leyland Tiger PS1. New to Southdown in 1948 (1287), the Beadle-bodied coach was withdrawn twelve years later and headed for Leigh in Lancashire where it was converted to a travelling shop by 'J.S.B. The Grocer'. (Author's Collection)

Opposite above: Surely the ultimate in travelling grocers' shops, with two 'sales floors'! A Leyland PD3 new to Leicester as 208, the double-decker remained on its old stomping ground thanks to the ingenious conversion by Belco Supermarkets. (Author's Collection)

Opposite below:Fitted with modern indicators on the front section, CCK 486 was a former Ribble Bedford OB which was bought and operated by A. Thomas in Skewen, South Wales as a mobile shop. This view dates from March 1974. (Mike Street)

Another Bedford OB which ended life in the Welsh valleys! HOD 64 was new in 1949 to Western National as fleet No.2013. Officially described as a 'semi-chassisless' B40R bus by John C. Beadle of Dartford, the 'Star Value Foodstore' is caught on camera in 1979 near Duffryn. The Monk family from Bridgend bought the bus in the early years of the next decade with restoration in mind, but a change in circumstances led to 'Jeremy' (because it was a Beadle!) being sold to Crumlin Auto Salvage.

This unidentified Bedford WTB is arguably the furthest-travelled mobile shop! Thomas Maclellan was based in Castlebay on the island of Barra in the Outer Hebrides, off the west coast of Scotland. The destination blind appears to show 'Both Trains', suggesting this vehicle started service on the UK mainland. Judging by the coach's condition shown in this 1960s image, it is fair to assume the last customer was served some time previous! It is believed this vehicle was part of a twenty-strong batch of WTBs with Duple bodies delivered new to W. Alexander in 1936 (W32–W51 WG4426-37 and WG4546–4553). (R.L. Grieves Collection)

Chateau Catering brought fine dining on wheels in the shape of former Biss Bros, Bishop Stortford HNK 150G. The Plaxton-bodied AEC Reliance was new in 1969. (Author's Collection)

Two former London Transport vehicles serving the film/TV industry in their later lives. *Above*: Park Royal bodywork was carried by this Leyland Atlantean. New in 1978 as London Country AN180, the double-decker was purchased by Film Flow in 1995 and was still in use as a dining unit in 2005, when the upper deck was damaged by fire. *Below*: No.498 in LT's 'SM' Class, the distinctive-looking MCW B41D+ 19 standees AEC Swift also operated for London Country. Seen here in Livingston's Catering colours, the single-decker is reported as still existing with Willie's Wheels, a company which specialises in supplying a diverse variety of vehicles to the film and TV sector in the UK and Europe. (Both Author's Collection)

This vehicle was a third-hand purchase for the catering operator. Bought new by East Kent (8827) in April 1982, the Leyland Leopard with ECW body headed north to become No.827 with Lancaster City Transport in the early 1990s. (Author's Collection)

This Leyland single was de-Nationalised after public service! The registration is obviously not the original, which created difficulties in trying to discover the vehicle's original operator. Now owned by well-known seafood specialists Crystal Waters of Lowestoft, the single-decker is a familiar sight around Suffolk, and has been dubbed 'Big Marlin III'. (Author's Collection)

3

TRANSPORT(ER)S OF DELIGHT!

Single-deck buses – and coaches in particular – became popular in the second half of the twentieth century with those whose sporting pursuits involved horse-power of contrasting range! With seats removed, a ramp added and other necessary conversions made, an old coach changed from a people carrier to a vehicle carrier, for stock-cars, rally cars motorcycles and other allied high-powered racing machines. More often than not the 'transporter' element did not take up the entire length of the coach, with the front section retained for living accommodation whilst travelling, or at least seating/resting facilities. Similarly, many equestrian lovers saw the sense, and economy, in transforming vehicles into horse-boxes with built-in sleepover space, etc.

The vehicles featured in the following photographs all had their lives prolonged by such conversions, albeit some underwent major surgery in the process!

New to Ribble in 1969, this Plaxton-bodied Leyland Leopard served with Lincolnshire as an NBC coach. It is seen here in the ownership of Surrey-based Renault franchise SMC, who sponsored and supported father-and-son duo Jim Edwards Senior and Junior for some years. (Author's Collection)

An ECW/Bristol RE with C38Ft body, this single-decker was new to Scottish Omnibuses/ Eastern Scottish, and retained the operator's livery when acquired by the Brora Motocross team. (Author's Collection)

Even after conversion, Plaxton coachwork can be recognised on this Bedford vehicle which had been new to Warner of Milford. It remained in south-west Wales with the new owners. It is not clear if 'The Lady Louise' under the windscreen refers to the former coach, or to the fine four-legged filly it carries! (Author's Collection)

No sleeping space in this stock-car coach by the look of it! BNO 114B was a 1964 Bedford SB13, with Duple (Northern) Firefly bodywork, built at the former Burlingham works in Blackpool, essentially to a Burlingham design. It was new to Eastern National as a forty-one-seater, stock number 505, and sold in 1970 to Cropley of Fosdyke in Lincs. Some time later it was acquired by BriSCA F1 driver Brian Tuplin. BriSCA is the British Stock Car Racing governing body. (Author's Collection)

Making a visit to the Scottish Vintage Bus Museum Open Weekend in 1997, GSN 411E was still on the road at the age of thirty, in the guise of a horsebox. The Ford R192 with Plaxton Panorama coachwork was new to Barries of Balloch who operated as Loch Lomond Coaches. (Author's Collection)

Caetano started building wooden-framed bus/coach bodies back in 1946, and nine years later became the first company in Portugal to use all-steel construction. In 1971 their bodies were imported into the UK and affixed to various chassis. Caetano's contemporary body-shape is still recognisable on BBH 813K, a Ford coach which was new to Williams of Buckingham, despite the extensive transformation to car-carrier for the unknown Suzuki motorcycle racing team. (Author's Collection)

This Bedford VAL70 ended up conveying the heaviest of all horsepower – Shires. The vehicle is pictured in Cardiff in 1986 with Mike Horler, but the twin-steer coach started life in Cornwall fifteen years earlier with Stoneman of Nanpean. (Mike Street)

Two views of coach conversions with the transporter section being open platform. *Above*: In the leafy avenue near Cardiff Museum, this Duple Viceroy-bodied Bedford VAM was operating for Simon Nevline's Transporter Hire business. (Mike Street) *Below*: Seddon Pennine 4 was new to Billies of Mexborough, and in the 1980s moved to Welsh operator Jones of Llansilin. The vehicle originally carried Plaxton Elite fifty-three-seat bodywork, some of which remains evident in its last role as a transporter/support vehicle for British Truck Racing. (Author's Collection)

The French Riviera may well have been a destination for this Leyland Tiger Cub in its heyday with Spencers of Manchester, but the 1959 Duple Britannia coach spent its senior days with the 'Saltyres' car-racing team in Scotland. (Author's Collection)

With contemporary Alexander bodywork, this Volvo B58 was operated by Western SMT on the Scotland-England 'trunk' routes, including Glasgow to London. After clocking up many motorway miles, the single-decker has since been put to good use as a transporter-cum-caravan by Tony Jordan, the well-known vintage vehicle collector from Leicester. The normal 'passenger' for HSD 709N is a finely restored Scammel Scarab. As with his collection, the Volvo coach is well cared for by its owner, and was still to the fore in 2008. (Author's Collection)

4

EXHIBITIONISTS

If you strip a double-deck bus of its seating, the 'floor-space' on each deck is quite substantial, certainly sufficient capacity to enable the vehicle to be used for exhibition and promotional purposes. That was the concept put in place by some smart person or persons (unknown), probably in the 1960s, and the idea caught on and was undertaken by businesses and other commercial companies, charities, and even local authorities.

Single-deckers also fulfil this role, and I have included a couple of particularly ingenious conversions – at least in my humble opinion! On display in this chapter are a variety of vehicles, some of which are still 'showing off'!

Modes on the move in the shape of former Eastern National Bristol FLF (2920).
The double-decker, owned by West Yorkshire-based Changes Fashions, is pictured in the early 1980s. This was not the last 'change of (ad)dress' this bus would make. It moved to the Continent and was refitted with seats by Antique Auto, near Brussells, and was last recorded there in 2004. (Author's Collection)

Among the last batch of Leyland Atlanteans delivered new to London Transport, JPJ 284W has certainly been around the country. In 1988 it joined the Drawlane fleet, and was re-branded London & Country the following year. Nine years on, and the Roe-bodied double-decker was bought by Arriva Surrey and West Sussex, before passing to Manchester 'indie' Finglands months later. Final PCV service was in the East Yorkshire fleet (397) from 1997–2004, and then till the following year with EYMS, before being snapped up by the *Jobs & Training Weekly* publication as a promotional vehicle. (Author's Collection)

This Bristol RELL was new in 1969 as UHU 215H with ECW B44D bodywork. After twelve years' service with Bristol Omnibus Company, the bus was purchased by Kodak at Ruislip and converted to a display unit. In the summer of 1982 it passed to Basingstoke Furniture, and by 1985 had been sold off to Wigley, the Carlton dealer/breaker, for scrap. (Author's Collection)

An extremely articulate(d) bus, CRM 927T was originally a Leyland National 'bendy-bus' demonstrator. The vehicle is still to the fore, now owned by D. Chambers from Exeter. (Author's Collection)

Another mobile gallery in the sunshine. A Leyland PD3/A new to BMMO in 1966 (2007), the Willowbrook-bodied bus crossed to the Isle of Man in 1972, becoming No.70 in the Road Services fleet. Four years later, retaining the same fleet number, the double-decker moved in to the Isle of Man Transport Ltd ranks, and, when it had finished carrying islanders and tourists round Ellen Vannin, was converted to a gallery-on-wheels, still under Manx Government ownership. (Author's Collection)

A Park-Royal-bodied Daimler Fleetline, this bus was new in the autumn of 1971 to West Midlands PTE as No.4103. Two decades on saw the vehicle with some seating still in place and partially open-topped, working as an exhibition/hospitality unit for Freedom Fuels. (Author's Collection)

Opposite above: New in 1938 as London Transport's Green Line T506, this AEC Regal passed via North the dealer in 1954 to Jones & Stephany of North London, who used the single-decker as a mobile upholstery showroom. (Chris Stanley Collection)

Opposite below: Former East Midland Motor Services C97 was transformed by Cowan Office Equipment Ltd into a showroom/exhibition unit. The Bristol RELH was still to the fore in this wintry 1990s shot. (Author's Collection)

Two RT's a continent apart in their twilight years. *Above*: Formerly KXW 102, and still showing its London Transport fleet number on the bonnet, RT 2473 navigates a fountain-cum-roundabout in Barcelona. This bus was recorded as still being with Promobus of Madrid in 2008, but sold off by August that year. In this view, the AEC double-decker is in the guise of mobile showroom for Philips Video/Computer technology. The Weymann-bodied RT was exported to Spain way back in 1967. *Below*: This AEC Regent III started life as RT 3882 (LLU 681). The classic bus is pictured in the capital after stage-carriage service, as a mobile exhibition unit for Hilti Power Tools and Fastenings, who were celebrating twenty-five years in this view from 1983. Far from being the last role, RT 3882 became a 'film star' when it was one of three ex-LT RTs converted to 'triple-deckers' to play the 'Knight Bus' in the *Harry Potter* series of movies. (Both Author's Collection)

Electronic Arts (EA) is the world's leading independent developer and publisher of interactive entertainment and games software for console systems. In the early part of the new millennium, the company used UWW 512X as part of their 'big in the game' promotion. The Alexander-bodied Metrobus was new to West Yorkshire PTE, and then passed to Classic Coaches of Annfield Plain, Co. Durham. (Author's Collection)

New to Nottingham Corp. in 1965 (No.463), this Metro-Cammell seventy-six-seat Atlantean headed to the South West after withdrawal, when bought by Amber, a charity dealing with unemployed under-thirties. It was originally destined for conversion by the Teacher Training Association for recruitment 'roadshows', however they apparently did not use it and the Amber Foundation purchased the bus in 2002 from the London Bus Co., Lydney, Forest of Dean. The double-decker was sold some five years later to a 'private collector' in Melksham. (Author's Collection)

Apart from the RT, the iconic 'London Bus' is the Routemaster. The vehicle in this picture is one of the city's RML class, i.e. with 30ft-long body. The additional bay increased the seating capacity from sixty-four to seventy-two. New to Aldenham Garage in 1967, RML 2670 enjoyed a long service life, passing into the privatised London General ranks, refurbished and refitted with an Iveco engine, before withdrawal in 2005. Purfleet dealer Ensign then sold on the Routemaster to the Government Communications network, who had it converted into a drugs abuse information bus, under the banner of 'Talk to Frank'. In 2008 the colour scheme was changed to light blue. (Author's Collection)

PVT 231L was new to Potteries Motor Traction Co. Ltd, a subsidiary of the National Bus Company (NBC), in December 1972, receiving fleet number 231. At some point during 1986 or 1987 it was sold to West Riding, who re-registered the bus 544 WRA. Before disposing of the bus West Riding re-registered it to FWW 215L, transferring its cherished registration to a Leyland Olympian. The bus was then acquired by Kirklees Metropolitan Borough Council in May 1990 who used it as a hospitality unit. It was subsequently sold to Ideas in Motion Ltd of Curragh, Eire, where it is used as a Mobile Exhibition unit. The bus has now been re-registered to ZV 8016. (Author's Collection/ Above right Ed O'Neil)

5

COMMUNITY SERVICE

Normally associated with fiscal punishment for miscreants who have committed misdemeanours, I have adopted the phrase 'community service' as an 'umbrella' for the buses and coaches featured in the following pages. This section is in many ways a natural sequel to the previous chapter on display/exhibition vehicles, but in these cases their purpose is linked with their local communities, in some shape or form.

The parameters are wide, from crime/fire prevention units and ambulances to mobile libraries and beauty treatments! From the latter decades of the twentieth century, local authorities and government departments have used second-hand buses as the ideal vehicle to take their services, campaigns, appeals and schemes out into the areas they serve, and have the flexibility of being able to move them around their respective regions. A couple of the older images illustrate this practice being deployed even before the 'swinging sixties'.

Parked at a shopping centre in 2007, HCF 183W takes NHS Greater Manchester's 'stop smoking' campaign to the public. A year later, the same vehicle is across in Newcastle deployed by another government agency! The double-decker, which has had a rear-end conversion on the upper deck, is an MCW Metrobus new to Reading in 1981 as No.183. (Above left Author's Collection/Above right Alastair Speight)

New to London (Regional) Transport in 1982, this all-Leyland Titan is well known in some parts! A regular participant at rallies, especially Showbus at Duxford, this double-decker has served Cambridgeshire Constabulary as both a mobile crime prevention unit and as a mobile police station. The bus has been 'immortalised' in the latter role as a model by EFE in 2003. (Author's Collection)

With archetypal chequered band, FHW 160D had not strayed too far from its old stomping ground when bought by Avon & Somerset Constabulary. The FLF6B was ex-Bristol O.C. No.C7255, and is pictured at the Bristol Rally in 1990. The bus was to enjoy a further lease of life when released from police custody – it passed to Piccadilly Tours at Winterthur in Switzerland and was last sighted there in 2007! (Author's Collection)

A 'weel Kent' double-decker which has been in the county for over thirty years. New to Maidstone & District in December 1973, the Bristol VRT ended stage service fifteen years later. Purchased by the Kent County Constabulary, it was converted to a Crime Prevention Unit, initially based in the Medway area, before being transferred to Canterbury in 1993. (Author's Collection)

There's no undercover police role for this 'Y'-type-bodied Leyland Leopard! New in 1973 to Alexander (Fife) as FPE 43, the single-decker was 'taken into custody' by the local constabulary after withdrawal from service and remained in the 'Kingdom'. The vehicle is basically still in Fife's cream/Ayres red waistband colours, but has the obligatory addition of a blue light and appropriate title in the destination screen. (Gordon Stirling)

Nowadays, most unitary authorities operate purpose-built travelling libraries, but in the past old single-deckers have been used as book-buses. *Above*: With a backdrop of terraced houses, HD 5827 is parked-up to serve readers in perhaps a mining village in Co. Durham. The Leyland Tiger had been new in 1936 to Yorkshire Woollen, and fitted with a thirty-two-seat Roe body. (Author's Collection) *Below*: Still wearing Sheffield Corp. Transport livery, this Leyland has been (easily) converted into a mobile library. New in January 1950, it was one of eight buses. Nos 56 and 61 were owned by STD and the others – 57-60/62-3 – were owned by British Railways; all were in Category 'B'. They were DP34R when new and in April 1962 No.56 was converted to a mobile library for the Sheffield Corporation Libraries, the work done in the Queens Road Works. It served for a number of years and was finally scrapped in 1978, after use as an office at a Barnsley scrapyard. (Author's Collection)

Northampton Borough Council made a neat conversion of this Willowbrook-bodied Daimler into a Community Bus. The bus was new to the city's Municipal Fleet as No.6 in 1973 with double-door forty-five-seat body. (Author's Collection)

New as London Transport's DMS 428, this 1972 Daimler double-decker was acquired in 1988 by Ringwood Public Address Service. This view shows the bus in its last years, providing a tannoy system for a promenade/beach event/fair at perhaps Southend-on-Sea or Brighton. The vehicle was scrapped in 2003. (Author's Collection)

Two images which could just as easily have featured in the 'mobile shops' section, but I considered them more apt for this chapter! *Above*: A Mark I Leyland National which has seen more hairs than fares for some years. The suitably coloured mobile men's hairdressing salon is permanently parked up on an area of the South Mimms Services, off the M25 at Potters Bar. The bus was No.ENL 853 in the Crossville fleet and carried DP49F body when new in 1974. (Author's Collection) *Below*: Another Leyland barber's bus, this Lynx began life in 1986 in Scotland as Kelvin Scottish 1101. The fifty-seven-seater also served Midland Red and Stevenson's of Uttoxeter and is captured here at its regular trading-place at Trowbridge, near Cardiff. (Author's Collection)

Staying on the theme of mobile makeovers ... the Beauty Bus is open for business at a regular 'pitch' just outside Birmingham's Rag market, offering a range of treatments and therapies. The former Nottingham Leyland Lion was one of the high-capacity eighty-eight-seaters with East Lancs bodywork supplied new in January 1989.

A South Yorkshire Atlantean which migrated south to become a Fire Prevention/Exhibition Unit with Kent Fire Brigade. The all-Leyland double-decker was No.1577 in the S.Y.P.T.E. ranks, and originally the second door was a central fixture. (Vernon C. Smith)

Opposite above: Promoting fire safety among the community in Nottinghamshire, this bus wears an appropriate all-red livery. The Bristol VRT was a series II model RCH 638L which had been No.776 in the Trent Motor Traction fleet. Later acquired by Trewoon TV, a television/video sales and service company in Cornwall, the vehicle was last reported in their ownership in 2007. (Author's Collection)

Opposite below: Two single-deck vehicles which converted from carrying fare-paying passengers to becoming ambulance buses. New to North Western Road Car in 1938 as No.940, this Bristol LS6G had its original ECW body replaced by a thirty-five-seat Burlingham version in 1950, and was re-numbered 376. Withdrawn in 1961, this view of the bus dates from the same decade. The owner of the ambulance is indistinct, and a Bristol 'sister' parked behind is on constabulary duties at a public event held possibly in a railway station/goods yard. (Author's Collection)

Childhood memories are evoked by the closing images in this chapter. Growing up in industrial Lanarkshire in the early 1960s, the imminent arrival of Christmas was not only heralded by wintry weather, but (normally) old buses parking up at the cul-de-sac end of our street. Royal Mail hired/acquired these vehicles as mobile sorting offices and parcel delivery stations, as well as providing some temporary respite for the poor posties who seemed to deliver cards and parcels constantly during any weekday when the festive rush was in full swing. Attempts to source Scottish images proved frustrating and fruitless, but since it was a role in which Royal Mail deployed vehicles all across the country, it is fitting to include this pair of ex-Eastern National fleet-members *Above*: XB 940 was still in Eastern National ownership when snapped at Southend. The full-fronted Bristol LL6 coach was new to Thomas Tilling in 1952, before becoming Eastern National EN 2201 eleven years later. Ironically, the 'XB' registration mark was also allocated to the Burgh of Airdrie and Coatbridge, Lanarkshire during the 1950s/60s! *Below*: Another Bristol, of 1951 vintage, wearing Eastern National colours whilst on Royal Mail duty two days before Christmas 1964. (Both Author's Collection)

6

CARAVANS AND LIVING ACCOMMODATION

Most people of a certain age will be familiar with the 1963 British film *Summer Holiday*, in which a youthful Cliff Richard and his chums take an old London Transport RT to Europe on a continental vacation. An ageing omnibus being used in such a way was actually true-to-life, and for many living 'on board' on a more permanent basis was also a reality, be it through circumstances or choice of lifestyle.

Arguably, converting an old bus or coach, especially single deck, is the most obvious and oldest change-of-use. Showmen and fairground operators have used ex-PSVs for decades, and their vehicles are rightly spotlighted in the closing chapter of this book! There have been generations of travelling-folk who have used an assortment of transport. Horse-drawn apart, the majority would tow a conventional caravan with an old lorry or van, but some turned to withdrawn buses as ideal homes.

From the 'Flower Power' era of the late 1960s' 'hippies' to twenty-first-century New Age travellers, many have found shelter and home comforts within the confines of an old coach, and of course they could easily accommodate families, groups etc., for their lives on the road. According to 'veteran' Dave, the traveller movement began in the late 1960s as the festival scene developed and grew in the mid-1970s, but was still low key until the early 1980s when a national tabloid newspaper brought it to the notice of the general public, after which things were never the same as more folks joined in. By the mid-1990s, internal problems saw most folks returning to static living.

The majority of the older vehicles have been scrapped, though some still linger at the bottom of people's gardens and a very small number still move around.

'Ordinary' people also turned to sold-off buses as an ideal way to acquire a vehicle which could be fairly inexpensively converted into a mobile holiday home for driving the wife and kids across the UK, and indeed further afield.

In a contrasting 'coffee-and-cream' colour scheme, JHL 716 makes a striking caravan, as the owner appears to carry out some routine maintenance. The 1956 Roe-bodied AEC Reliance was new to West Riding (716). (Author's Collection)

A real case of 'keeping it in the family' with this bus! One of twenty Daimler CVD6s delivered to the famous North East Independent Venture Bus Co. between 1946 and 1948, JPT 544 is the sole survivor. When withdrawn from service, the company themselves converted it into a mobile caravan for employees and their families to take on their holidays, in which role it served well for many years. Found in a sorry state behind a London pub by enthusiast Ted Heslop, the first steps to preservation were taken. The Willowbrook-bodied single-decker (left, below) was fully restored by Michael Reed, the son of Jack, one of the founding brothers. On Michael's passing, his son did use the bus (it was popular for weddings/private hires), but he then sold it on. In 2009 it was believed to be still extant in the Co. Durham area. (Left above R.F. Mack/Left below P. Logie Coll.)

One of the most iconic British coach chassis of all time was Bedford's VAL, introduced at the 1962 Commercial Motor Show, the first time that Bedford ventured into the large-capacity coach market. Employing a vertically mounted Leyland engine, a low-height chassis, 16in wheels and a twin-steer front axle, it became the coach of its era. This 1967 example with fifty-two-seat Duple body has led a long and chequered life, starting with Morris of St Thomas. With several other owners, including use as a hospitality unit, the VAL was latterly converted to a caravan in the Oxford area by 2004. (Author's Collection)

Despite the blind display, this 1966 Ford is a long way from East Glamorgan Hospital – it is in a roadside campsite at Smeeton Westerby in Leicestershire. The photo was taken in 1994 when the bus was owned by travellers Jonathon and Clare. The Marshall-bodied vehicle was new to Bebb, South Wales. (Traveller Dave/www.travellerhomes.co.uk)

EO 5031 was a Leyland TS3 Tiger / Leyland B32R new to Barrow-in-Furness Corporation as No.10 in 1931, rebodied by East Lancs in 1943, and withdrawn in 1949. In this 1950s view the bus has obviously been bought and converted by someone who loves travelling in the great outdoors. The Latin motto *Semper Sursum*, used by many schools and institutions, means 'forever upward'. The smaller initials above are RAC for the Royal Automobile Club, and CC indicating the Caravan Club. The FDMC may well be some sort of Motorists/Motoring Club. (Author's Collection)

With family on board, the new owner of this ex-North Western Tiger cub gets away from it all in his new holiday-home-on-wheels. The forty-four-seat Weymann-bodied bus dates from 1957 and was No.685 in the North Western ranks, withdrawn in 1969. The little boy in the nearside section of the windscreen would surely pass for a real-life 'Joe 90', bearing a likeness to the character in the contemporary TV puppet series by Gerry Anderson! (Author's Collection)

The Bristol LS (light saloon) was a joint venture between Bristol Commercial Vehicles and Eastern Coach Works/W. Alexander, producing an 'integral' bus or coach, between 1951 and 1958. Still in its only PSV operating livery of United Counties Omnibus Co., Northampton, PNV 220 is parked up with a new owner in Stockport who bought the single-decker in 1975 and carried out the conversion to a caravan. The 1957 vehicle carried fleet nos 120 and latterly 441 with United Counties, and was finally scrapped in 1980. (Author's Collection)

VWM 89L was already 'preserved' and regularly on rally duty when it was bought by Brian Weller. In 2006, the Oxfordshire family decided to escape the rat race, and undergo a complete lifestyle change, and thus ex-Southport 89 was expertly transformed into a motor-home, including solar roof panels (see www.usonthebus.com for the full story). After two years of a 'nomadic' existence, the family brought the Leyland Atlantean back to England, and moved back into a fixed four-walls-and-roof home. (Author's Collection)

Former Gardiner's of Spennymoor, Co. Durham converted to a caravan. The Ford Thames coach had Burlingham's uncommon 'Gannet' style of bodywork. (Author's Collection)

Opposite page: Two AEC coaches which worked in England but are captured on camera in Glasgow in their 'retirement' days as caravans. *Above*: This rather unusual vehicle is not an AEC Reliance, but a Regal IV underfloor-engined chassis, No. 9821E1435. Built in May 1952 for Johnson of Stourbridge, the bodywork (C41C) was built by Heaver of Durrington (near Salisbury). (A.J. Douglas) *Below*: Reliance 165 BML was new to Venture Transport in 1954 and carried stylish C41C body by Duple. (Author's Collection)

This section on mobile living would not be complete without including Top Deck Travel, surely the consummate converter of buses to caravans, for sojourns into Europe, Africa and other continents. Aimed at the eighteen-thirties age group, the London-based company, which is still very much to the fore, started acquiring Bristol double-deckers in the late 1970s, initially Lodekkas, then VRs and single-deck REs and MWs. The cream/orange/black livery was striking, and each vehicle was given a name, which was painted on the vehicle. Having carried thousands of passengers in the UK on stage-carriage duties, most of these vehicles clocked up many more miles with Top Deck. *Above*: New to Southern Vectis (537) in 1955, LDL 736 is pictured on Top Deck duty in Amsterdam in the early 1990s. The LD6G, nicknamed 'Befa', had to be scrapped in 1995 after its front axle was ripped out in an accident in Iran of all places! (Author's Collection) *Below*: Acquired from Western National in 1980, 'Edgar' served his new owners for some sixteen years, and the FLF fell victim to the blowtorch after suffering roof damage. Parked alongside is GAE 881D, 'Tutai', a former Bristol and West Riding bus. (Author's Collection)

This MCCW-bodied Leyland PD2 was new in 1966 to Salford, and became GMPTE GMT3103. Bought by a local dance troupe after withdrawal, the bus then passed to a traveller, in whose ownership it is seen in 1992 on a site at Wansford. (Traveller Dave)

A Welsh Tiger Cub which roamed free after service life in the Valleys. New in 1957 to James of Ammanford, Aberavon, the Leyland single-deck was absorbed into the South Wales Transport fleet as firstly No.808 (below) and then as No.312. The bus was built with a Weymann B44F body. (Author's Collection/Below Mike Street)

Barratt Homes – the housebuilder developed out of the original company Greensitt & Barratt
– enjoyed a high-profile marketing campaign in the 1980s and early '90s, with TV adverts
featuring helicopters. Carrying the trademark oak tree logo, 780DAU was a Leyland Titan PD3/1
from 1959 with MCW bodywork. New to Skills, Nottingham as No.80, it had been with OK
Motor Services of Bishop Auckland before reaching Barratt. It is seen here in July 1974 at the
Mallowdale, Nunthorpe, Middlesbrough site. (Donald Hudson)

Wearing the colours and signage of construction amalgum Balfour Beatty-Fairclough, GRM
300L was new in 1974 to Cumberland, part of the NBC. (Author's Collection)

Captured in May 1988 at the Claerwen Dam in South Wales, 324 FOF was a Plaxton-bodied Bedford SB5 coach from 1962. (Mike Street)

Still going places at forty-plus years of age! ASC 671B was new to Edinburgh Corporation in 1964 in a fifty-strong batch of Titan PD3/6s with Alexander H41/29F bodies. Looking immaculate in the summer of 2008, the bus was actually in the middle of a tour of the UK and Republic of Ireland. CoaguNation is an educational resource provided by Roche Diagnostics in collaboration with Anticoagulation Europe, a registered charity committed to giving support to patients, their families and carers on all aspects of anticoagulation therapy. The venue was the New Mersey Retail Park at Speke, Liverpool. The writing above the radiator slats reads: 'On Hire from the London Bus Export Coy' who actually own the classic marque. (Courtesy of Roche Diagnostics)

Starting life in Ayrshire, this Bedford SB coach enjoyed a musical retirement as a mobile organ studio/showroom in Wales. (Mike Street)

The distinctive contemporary 'wavy' grille means Bristol – RELH6G to be precise, with forty-seven coach seats by ECW, and new to United Welsh in 1964. Caught on camera nineteen years later at a rally, the vehicle is owned by Cortina Windows, but is on charitable duty raising cash for a Sunshine Coach for the Variety Club of Great Britain, backed by TV sports presenter Gary Newbon. (Mike Street)

A Leopard which certainly changed its spots is NMS 186M. New to Alexander (Midland) as MPE 156, the single-decker fell into the ownership of Compass (Scotland) who provide training, development and stress management. 'Massage on the Move' is one of two mobile therapy vehicles operated by the company, the other being an ex-Tayside/Dundee Volvo Ailsa. (D.G. MacDonald)

A Leyland PS1 whose working life was spent in South Wales and lives on in preservation – at the second attempt! Bought by independent Griffin of Brynmawr in the summer of 1949, the bus became Red & White No.S1449 on takeover. Noted as with the local Voluntary Welfare Association five years previously, this 1974 photo shows the vehicle still in the Rhondda, but now with the Multiple Sclerosis Society. Restored to Red & White colours by 1977, the Lydney coachwork-bodied bus was with a private owner in Chepstow, where it lay in an open driveway for nearly twenty-eight years, and whose condition deteriorated as a result. Thankfully, in 2005 a small group of members of the Cardiff Transport Preservation Group purchased the bus and removed the Leyland from its 'residence' in 2006; they have since successfully returned it to pristine, preserved condition. (Mike Street)

Still in full livery, but minus fleet names, this ex-Western SMT Daimler Fleetline looks as
if it was only withdrawn shortly before this photo was taken in the north of Scotland.
The Alexander-bodied double-decker, which was No.1994 in the WSMT ranks, has had interior
work carried out to convert the 1965 bus to a two-storey house-on-wheels. (Peter Findlay)

In the words of the old Scottish song, this coach-caravan has taken the road and the miles to
Dundee. New in 1955 to John Carmichael's 'Highland' of Glenboig in Lanarkshire, the Albion
Victor with thirty-five-seat Duple body was acquired by Alexander (Midland) when they took over
the independent eleven years later. Numbered MNA 8 in the SBG operator's fleet, the vehicle was
withdrawn in 1967, and sold via Glasgow dealer Millburn Motors for private conversion. Fitting
for the Albion motto 'sure as the sunrise', the veteran Victor basks in the summer warmth in the
City of Discovery in 1977. (Don Hudson)

8855 LG was a Bedford SB with Yeates 'Pegasus' body new to Martin of Weaversham in Cheshire. Yeates 'FE44' – front-entrance forty-four seats – was the bodybuilder's modification to the SB chassis. The vehicle was last seen on the road in 1985, and scrapped in London two years later. (D.G. MacDonald)

This Willowbrook-bodied Fleetline was No. 542 in the Cardiff Municipal fleet, and when withdrawn was transferred to the South Glamorgan Playbus Association. It is seen here outside Cardiff City Hall in 1982. (Mike Street)

RFM 420 was among the first deliveries of Bristol Lodekka to Crossville Motor Services. From a total of forty-six supplied in 1954, ML675 was one of eight LD6Bs with ECW CH30/22 bodies, i.e. coach seating. The bus was withdrawn by 1971, and is pictured here the following summer in Aberavon, providing suitable transport for the Fochriw Mini-Paraders Jazz Band. (Mike Street)

A Guy Special new to London Transport in 1953 (GS14), this twenty-four-seat bus later passed to Ballets Minerva of Wembley, a touring dance company, and is caught on camera in September 1972 at Yarm-on-Tees. The vehicle was acquired for preservation four years later, moved to a new owner in 1986, and finally restored in 'London Country' green livery. (Don Hudson)

New to Blackpool Corp. (395), this Leyland PD3A1 is seen in Coatham, Redcar, the locale of its latter owners, the Redcar Marines JJB. The photo dates from 1979, when the bus, with Metro-Cammell body, was approaching fifteen years old. (Don Hudson)

Two peas in a pod would be apt for this pair of AEC Reliances, used by Lockwood Foods at their canning factory in Forfar, Angus. The coaches are Commer Avengers with Harrington Crusader bodies. (Peter Findlay)

Two mobile restaurants/hospitality units once used at motorsport and horse-racing events by 'Le Chien Qui Fume', a French restaurant in East Molesey. On the right, GRY 57D is a 1966 Leyland PD3 new to Leicester City Transport (57), but the bus on the left is the more interesting of the pair. Originally registered 8122 MN, the AEC Regent V was the first forward-entrance double-decker on the Isle of Man, as Douglas Corp. Trans No.1, entering service in 1964. In 1976 the bus became 122 (later re-numbered to 139) in the Isle of Man National Transport ranks. Withdrawn in 1982, it was bought by a Manx resident for preservation, sold in 1984 to Brakell the bus dealer in Cheam, from whom it was acquired two years later by the French cuisine company, and it was re-registered Q 825 PGT. It was last used by the 'Smoking Dog Event Catering' in 2005/6. The vehicle still has a Manx blind in place, judging by 'Quarter Bridge' being shown in this shot. (Author's Collection/inset RHG Simpson)

A true Lancashire bus. New to John Fishwick of Leyland, with East Lancs bodywork, this 1976 Leyland Atlantean was acquired in 2004 by Music Links, a music development charity for Cumbria based in Kendal. In December 2008, they sold the double-decker to the Royal Zoological Society of Scotland, who were converting it in 2009 to 'The Wild Bus' to take reptiles on tour throughout Scotland! (Author's Collection/Royal Zoological Society of Scotland)

Historically, the 'Auld Alliance' between Scotland and France dates back to the thirteenth century, but thankfully the connection for this image is much more recent. A travelling art gallery, the double-decker basks in the summer sun in the South of France. The 1967 FLF began life with Alexander (Fife) as FRD 213 (HXA 413E) in the final batch of Lodekkas delivered new to that operator. (Author's Collection)

New as West Yorkshire 1846, this Leyland Olympian later became No.314 in the Harrogate & District ranks. The bus was then bought by Sharon Telfrod and moved to Leeds to become a 'Kidzone' Party Bus. The owner had three buses at one time, but had to scrap two of them as they could not pass MoTs! (Author's Collection)

Not one but two chimney stacks on travellers' VRT/SL2 camped deep in woods in Herefordshire. The double-decker was new to Southdown (551) in 1973. Remarkably, the 'Please Pay As You Enter' sign on the front panel still appears to light up, but perhaps the request is only applicable to 'non-residents'! (Author's Collection)

New to City of Oxford in 1960. this Willowbrook-bodied AEC Reliance was later acquired by H. Payne Farms, near Maidstone in Kent. (Derek Jones)

This articulated Leyland National started life at Heathrow Airport as a British Airways 'shuttle-bus'. Later acquired by Government agencies, it has been a Jobs Bus in Lincolnshire, and then a mobile 'play and learn' centre under the 'Sure Start' banner. The 1981 vehicle still carries the flashing orange light required with its original owner. (Author's Collection)

Ultra was part of the Thorn Electrics group, and used several vehicles for staff at their television factory in Gosport. With stylish Duple Britannia C41C body, 444 BXD was new in 1961 to Samuelsons of London. (Author's Collection)

With no less than Ronald himself at the wheel, ex-LT Routemaster RM 1807 was originally registered 807 DYE in 1964. The fast food chain acquired the bus in 1992 and adapted it to become a party bus. The location in this view is in Manchester, but the bus was last sighted in 2003 in Clitheroe. (David Longbottom)

Another Olympian, but with a body by Chas H. Roe, which has led a colourful life. New to London Country as LR16 in 1982, the double-decker moved to Clydeside Scottish C1072 before heading back across the border into the Arriva North East fleet as 7263. After withdrawal, the bus crossed country to the North West, to be transformed into this smart party bus in Manchester. (Author's Collection)

The ultimate in early 'all-over' bus advertising? 972 EHW was new in 1959 to the Bristol Omnibus Co. (LC 8518). Withdrawn in 1976, it was sold via North's, the Sherburn dealer, to a farmer in Roxby before passing to Norton Strawberry Growers in whose colours it is seen here at Liverpool in June 1984. Following two other moves for preservation, the Lodekka was finally purchased around 2000 for further restoration by Dr Mike Walker and Alan Peters. (Author's Collection)

Former East Kent Guy Arab III remained in its home county, the 'Garden of England', after withdrawal and was used by Wey Street Fruit Farm at Faversham. This Park Royal double-decker, new in 1951, has also been restored to original condition, and is a rally regular. (Author's Collection)

Above and below: Latterly used as living accommodation (of sorts) by Ski Beach Villas in the Dolomites, MFN 948F began its working life with East Kent. The Park Royal-bodied AEC Regent V also served the company as a Driver Trainer before heading for the Italian Alps. (Author's Collection/below P. Esposito)

7

PLAY DAYS

By the end of the 1960s, a lot of 'green' land had been swallowed up for housing, both public and private. The trend was to continue into the following decade, with high-rise blocks of flats dotting the skylines, especially in the larger towns and cities. The construction of 'lower level' houses saw sprawling estates of council flats and homes form 'concrete jungles' in numerous suburbs. In some developments the provision of recreational areas for children was built into the project, but in the main this aspect was not a priority. Local authorities across the country developed the idea of providing mobile play facilities, particularly for younger children in socially deprived areas, be it on the newer estates or the older schemes. Play and interaction has been, and still is, regarded as an integral part of any child's development. Thus the 'Playbus' was born, with second-hand vehicles acquired either from authorities' own municipal fleets, from other operators or via dealers. They were duly converted into playgrounds-on-wheels, and were usually brightly decorated with multicoloured exteriors. Playbuses provided a valuable social service for twenty years or so, but with local and national government reform, and indeed many more working mothers, nursery facilities and early learning centres have had to be provided on a more permanent basis, both by the state and private enterprise. A few playbuses continue to operate, but are now in a minority compared to earlier years, and most of these are run by commercial businesses.

As the 1990s progressed, the idea of the 'Party Bus' evolved. Enterprising individuals and some companies saw a niche market for parents who liked the idea of being able to hire a mobile party venue for special occasions, birthdays etc., and indeed the adult version developed from the same lines.

Once again, used PCVs have provided the ideal vehicles to put the ideas into action. In the majority of cases, double-deck buses were the preferred option for obvious reasons of more space, capacity etc., but single-deckers have also been utilised.

London Transport also used Leyland chassis and hence the 'RTL' was born, and the bodies/chassis were inter-changeable between the AEC RT and Leyland RTL classes. Former RTL 592 is seen in Kilmarnock as the 'Rainbow Room' playbus, and by the look of the symbol in the destination screen is sponsored by the local Rotary Club. The bus is parked up in the shadow of Western SMT's main depot and HQ at Nursery Avenue. (Author's Collection)

Opposite above & below: Central SMT was a core member of the Scottish Bus Group, serving Lanarkshire and part of Dunbartonshire, and many withdrawn vehicles led extended lives with other owners, as illustrated here. B87 in the CSMT fleet, this Bristol LD6G was later acquired by Strathclyde Regional Council and converted to a playbus, operating throughout Lanarkshire. The double-decker was then bought by a private individual who parked the bus at his remote home as a play area for his own children. After lying in the outdoors for over a decade, the Lodekka was 'discovered' by the author, and eventually bought for preservation by a friend, who has restored it to its former glory. (Gordon Stirling)

The Bristol VR's performance and maintenance problems forced the Scottish Bus Group into a vehicle 'swap shop' in 1973 with their NBC counterparts, with the VRTs heading back south in exchange for late-model FLFs. New to Eastern Scottish (Scottish Omnibuses) in 1968 as AA300, the rear-engined double-decker joined the Southdown ranks, and after withdrawal moved into Essex to become the Chelmsford Play Bus. (Author's Collection)

An East Lancs-bodied Leyland National Greenway, GUW 459W entered service in November 1983 with London General (GLS459). The bus has been totally transformed in this guise as a Sensory Bus with Bright Beginnings Day Nursery in Balby, Doncaster. (Author's Collection)

Still to the fore in 2005, this Atlantean saw stage service with GMPTE and operating subsidiary Birkenhead & District. The bus had a seventy-five-seat body by NCME, before conversion to a playbus. (Author's Collection)

B905 XJO was one of a batch of five MCW Metrobuses delivered new to the City of Oxford in April 1985, with MCW CH53/23F bodies. The 'mega-decker' then became the South Holland Playbus in Lincolnshire. (Author's Collection)

The distinctive lines of Alexander bodywork are clearly evident on this Atlantean playbus. The Leyland double-decker was new in 1969 to Glasgow Corporation (and then GGPTE) as LA490. (Author's Collection)

P309 MLD was one of the first generation Dennis Darts for London Transport. The 9.8m bus was EDR 33 in the Metroline ranks. In 2007, the vehicle was sold to Qualiti Conversions in Hampshire who specialise in transforming buses and coaches into specialised vehicles. Their handywork has been expertly applied to the Dart, which is seen here at Port Erin on the Isle of Man, about to be 'officially unveiled' as a Youth Bus ... some poetic licence taken on the 'playbus' theme! (Author's Collection)

Party-Kids is a Driffield- (Yorks) based business specialising in children's mobile entertainment. 'Sid' is one of two double-deckers used and is a veritable 'fun palace' inside with soft play and adventure areas for younger kids. The vehicle, which was bought via the London Bus Export Co. and had been in Belgium, originally operated in Nottingham. Owner Dawn Simpson, who acquired the Leyland in 2002, says that the bus has been more reliable than 'Sylvia', an ex-Yorkshire Traction Bristol VRT from 1981, and she has insisted that when the time comes to retire 'Sid' he'll be converted into a family motor home! (Dawn Simpson)

8

DANCERS ON 'DECKERS ... AND MOBILE MUSICIANS

This chapter is, in many ways, a natural follow-on to the previous, with the principal theme being youngsters, fun and enjoyment. As with playbuses, someone, somewhere who was involved with children's majorettes and dancers decided to buy a second-hand bus or coach to transport their charges to competitions, displays and gala days, etc. The idea caught on, others soon followed, and from my photographic sources the concept of having customised transport really flourished in the 1970s and '80s.

Baton twirling majorettes, dance troupes and juvenile jazz bands were all very popular across England and Wales, with a seemingly heavy presence in the North East and North West. Regional and national contests were held, while the 'traditional' village fetes, gala day parades, summer shows and fair days were all outlets for the talented and colourful youngsters – from the 'tiny tots' to the teenagers – to perform at.

A used PSV, especially a double-decker, was the ideal vehicle not only to provide conveyance for these performers, but with even minimal conversion, also changing facilities and room to carry their array of costumes and outfits, and in the case of bands, their instruments. Aside from youthful entertainers, adult groups of performers also utilised old buses in a similar fashion, as can be seen in the following selection of images.

Coaching comfort was also the order of the day for the members of the Wellingborough Royal British Legion Majorettes. The forty-nine-seater was a Bedford YRT with Plaxton body which had been new in 1973 to Harris of Grays. (Author's Collection)

Opposite above: The Chelmsford Twirlettes acquired this NCME-bodied Daimler Fleetline, new to Southdown as No.2126 in September 1971. A colourful paint and decal job has been done for this battalion of baton twirlers, whose organisers also secure local sponsorship. (Author's Collection)

Opposite below: This AEC Reliance coach moved to Mansfield from its original Devon General operating territory (Fleet No.33). The Royston Diamonds Drum Majorettes are alighting from the Duple (Northern)-bodied vehicle, in readiness for another display. (Author's Collection)

Morris dancers on the move in a pair of multi-coloured machines! *Above*: A-Jay's Morris Dance Troupe from Bolton used ex-Fylde Borough Council No.82, a Leyland Atlantean new in 1975. (Author's Collection) *Below*: VTC503M was new to Lancashire United. The NCME-bodied Daimler Fleetline is pictured here in the ownership of the Hag Fold not-so-modest Morris Dancers who proclaimed to be 'Simply the Best'! In fairness, the troupe, based in an area of Atherton in Greater Manchester, have won many honours and celebrated their 30th Anniversary in 2007. (Author's Collection)

Arriving at the venue of another competition are the musicians of the Ward Green Grenadiers Juvenile Jazz Band from Barnsley. Their coach is well travelled – the 1969 Bristol RELH was ex-Western National 1458. (Don Hudson)

Two Alexander-bodied Daimler Fleetlines which started life in Scotland. *Above*: PAG 852H was new to Dodds of Troon (DT15), part of the AA Motor Services independent 'co-operative'. Bought by the Earls Colne Majorettes and Marching Band, the double-decker is smartly turned out in maroon and white. Judging by the trophy display in the lower-deck window, the Essex-based troupe had been picking up prizes galore. (Author's Collection) *Below*: The Sutton Sentinels Jazz Band's bus was former Dundee Corporation No.39, which had been new to the municipal operator in 1966. (Author's Collection)

From the 1970s, Bristol-born Kelvin Henderson always had cutting-edge musicians in his band. He was ultra-professional in his approach to transport as well. While many acts settled on a Transit van or similar vehicle, the performer bought this twenty-two-seat Bedford VAS with Plaxton coachwork, which had been bought new by Frames of London WC2. Later becoming a promoter, producer and radio presenter, Henderson was inducted into the British Country Music Hall of Fame in 2008. (Author's Collection)

Leigh Corporation bought this East Lancs-bodied AEC Renown in 1966. Later No.1 in the SELNEC fleet, the seventy-five-seat bus provided transport for the Blue Jays. (Author's Collection)

New in 1986 to Greater Manchester PTE as No.3218, this Leyland Olympian was then swallowed up in the ubiquitous 'First' group, initially in the First Rochdale ranks, and then First Bristol. The bus, which has H43/26F bodywork by Northern Counties, was eventually purchased by the Silver Gems Dance Troupe in Manchester. (Author's Collection)

9

RELIGION ON
THE ROAD

For centuries, preachers and followers of many faiths have moved across the country to spread the Good Word and the message of their particular doctrines. In modern times, this could mean standing on a street corner or in a public park, or inviting locals to a gathering in a village hall. Renowned American Evangelist Billy Graham had larger venues, including sports stadia, packed by thousands who wanted to hear him preach in the 1950s and '60s. Many of us will also have had visits to our doorsteps by Jehovah's Witnesses, or Mormons, members of the Church of the Latter Day Saints.

As the twentieth century moved into its last decades, some religious groups, and even 'conventional' churches, took a new approach by purchasing used PCVs, and being mobile among many communities, including inner cities. Vehicles have been used for ministry work, outreach buses or just simply providing free transport to ferry worshippers to their services. The latter concept is not new, as I can recall several churches in Central Scotland hiring coaches to provide free transport for parishioners in a bid to boost falling congregations, and Sunday School/Bible Class rolls.

Representing the 'Good News' group, this ex-West Midlands Atlantean is well-travelled with its new owners. The MCW-bodied double-decker has been caught on camera in Aberdeen. (Peter Findlay)

The Jesus Army (also known as the Jesus Fellowship Church) aims to be a contemporary expression of the historic Christian faith. The Jesus Army is particularly active with many in need, including homeless young people, prisoners and ex-prisoners and those involved in alcohol and drug abuse. The Northamptonshire-based Evangelical group, founded in 1969, have utilised cast-off buses for a number of years. Ex-London Transport DMS 294 (JGF 294K), a Daimler Fleetline, was new in 1972. (Author's Collection)

This image has the bus in the religious group's 'original' rainbow-striped colour scheme.
(Author's Collection)

A more recent, and stylish, acquisition was B145 GSC. The 1984 Leyland Olympian with
Alexander CH43/20F bodywork was CLL 145 in the Eastern Scottish (Scottish Omnibuses)
fleet. The picture above shows the double-decker in its latter livery of mainly all-white.
(Author's Collection)

This page: Associated Bus Ministries facilitate the operation of a fleet of specially converted buses which are adapted for a wide variety of projects, ranging from mobile youth groups to soup kitchens for the homeless and high-profile exhibition units for missions. Both examples shown here started stage-carriage life in Scotland. This Leyland Leopard had Alexander DP49F 'T'-type bodywork, and was new to Fife Scottish as FPE173, later becoming 273 in the Stagecoach Fife fleet. (Author's Collection/Donald Stirling)

This page: Originally MDS707P, this bus was LA1044 in the Greater Glasgow, then Strathclyde PTE, ranks. The Atlantean, which also carries an Alexander body, has taken part in bus rallies, notably Showbus, in ABM colours. Before being transformed into a carrier of 'Good News', the vehicle had a more mundane role as an exhibition bus for Qwikline Consumer Units (above). (Author's Collection)

'The Bus' was a one-man ministry concept by Mr John Shipton from Lancashire, who became a 'born again Christian' in 2000. He bought the NCME-bodied Atlantean from Blackpool Transport, and converted the lower deck into a coffee bar and drop-in centre, with the upstairs used for younger children's recreation. The outreach bus, pictured here at Atherton Market, was sold to a Huddersfield breaker in 2007. The double-decker had been new in 1978 to Hull Corporation, passed to Lytham St Annes who were absorbed into the Blackpool Transport fleet. (Author's Collection)

UWJ 281Y was new to South Yorkshire Transport in 1983 (SYT 2281). The Dennis Dominator with seventy-eight-seat Alexander body latterly ran for First Bristol (30430) before passing to Sheffield-based City Church. (Author's Collection)

The message is clear on this Bristol LD6G! The double-decker was new in 1960 to Red & White as 20 AAX. It was absorbed into the National Welsh fleet until 1977 when it was converted to a driver-trainer. The vehicle was re-registered several times, and as late as 1991 was incorporated in the revamped Red & White ranks, but never used. The ECW H33/27RD bus was bought by Cross Keys (Newport)-based Gospel Express in whose ownership it is seen here at a Carnival Day. In 1998, the bus passed to another Christian group and subsequently three other owners for preservation, the last of whom is fittingly the Revd Patrick Coleman of Abertillery (above right). The vicar of St Michael's also owns/part-owns two other preserved Welsh buses – ex-Jones Tiger Cub 889 AAX and TAX 235, another former R&W Lodekka. (Author's Collection/the Revd Patrick Coleman)

Atlantean UMR 195T was new in 1978 to Thamesdown as No.195. The ECW-bodied double-decker was purchased by the Vale Churches Youth Group from Faringdon in Oxfordshire. Converted to a Cyber Bus, the Group visited around five villages on a fortnightly basis. The vehicle was sold on and worked in Sliema, Malta, converted to an open-top sightseeing bus by Supreme Travel, and was still being used in 2009. (Author's Collection)

A long-life Lodekka, which entered service in 1966 with Eastern Counties (FLF473). Withdrawn at the age of twenty, the Gardiner-engined FLF was bought by the Church Army Evangelical Group and converted into a caravan/mission/recruitment bus, firstly painted in a maroon livery (above right) and latterly bright green with yellow relief. (Author's Collection)

The coach seating in this former Eastern Scottish 'Y'-type Bedford YRQ made it an ideal vehicle for the Larne Congregational Church to use to provide transport for the Irish parishioners. (Author's Collection)

10

FRUIT-PICKING PASSENGERS

Time-expired vehicles were used by farmers to transport temporary farm workers from towns and cities. They were particularly popular with fruit farmers in Perthshire/Tayside where berries are the principal summer crop – hence the name 'berry buses' – but vehicles were often used in a similar way by commercial potato growers. Fellow producers in Kent, and those who grew hops and apples, may also have used withdrawn PSVs in a similar fashion, but the main deployment was unquestionably in Scotland. The harvesting of both crops was labour intensive, and required seasonal workers. In many cases, generations of families would take paid holidays out of berry-picking or 'tattie-howking' (potato picking).

The use of buses in this way began to decline from the 1980s onwards for a variety of reasons, among them the tightening up of driving and maintenance legislation, and the growing use of foreign labour on farms. The ultimate benefit of such buses to the growing preservation movement is that it helped to ensure the continued existence and restoration of a substantial number of vehicles that might otherwise have fallen victim to the breaker's blowtorch.

Whilst a number of the photographs in this section were taken in Scotland, all of the vehicles, with one exception, originated with English operators. The most recent image dates from 1993, but by then berry buses were becoming as rare as hen's teeth!

Peter Arbuckle's farm is in Invergowrie near Dundee. The fruit producer used this pair of AEC double-deckers. This Bridgemaster was new in 1959 to South Wales Transport (1199). Passing to Foster of Dinnington, the Park Royal-bodied bus was bought by Rennie's of Dunfermline in 1974, before moving from Fife to Tayside a couple of years later. (A.H. Dodsley)

217 AJF took a similar route to Arbuckle's, but began life in 1961 with Leicester City Transport, part of the first low-height double-deckers in that municipal fleet (217). When the bus served no further purpose on the farm, it was sold off to the well-known Scottish breaker Dunsmore of Larkhall, Lanarkshire. However, this AEC was spared the graveyard, and was rescued for restoration by the '217 Group'. Arbuckle's fruit-growing business is still extant, and locals and visitors alike can buy fruit in season from their farm shop.

Two former Yorkshire Traction Leylands which ended up ferrying fruit-pickers. *Above*: HHE 323 started life as AHE 467, a PS1 single-decker, but was rebodied by Roe in 1955 with a H33/26R body, renumbered 1042 in the 'Tracky' ranks, and re-registered. Along with five others from the same batch, the bus was bought by north-east independent Simpson of Rosehearty, near Fraserburgh. A year later the operator was taken over by Alexander (Northern) and this vehicle became NRA 106. Withdrawn in 1971, the Leyland was originally acquired by a Forfar farmer before being passed on to Fergusons. (Peter Findlay) *Below*: A PD3A model from 1962, XHE 229 carried Yorkshire Traction fleet number 1229. The 'destination' carried by the NCME seventy-three-seater is the name of the farm premises near Carnoustie where the bus ultimately worked for owner Andrew Gray. Judging by the sleeper jammed under the front wheel, some work on the brakes may have been required when this snap was taken! (P. Hanwell)

Still in full Western SMT livery, MSD 411 (D1547) worked on the farm of F.G. Pierce & Sons, Borough Green, Kent, between 1977 and 1982 (when they sold it to David Hoare at Chepstow). The all-Leyland bus with L35/32RD body had been new in July 1959. The fruit growers also had two other WSMT PD3s, D1518/29 (MSD 382/93). (Derek Jones)

The livery has been 'modified' but the fleet name and number are still visible on ex-Lancashire United Guy Arab, still working in 1993 on Redford's farm at Errol in Perthshire. The Northern Counties-bodied bus was later taken back to its former operating territory and has been preserved in full LUT glory.

The location and date are the same for this shot of former Derby 225, a Daimler Fleetline of 1969 vintage. The double-decker did head back to Derby when acquired by Harpurs, but was stripped for spares and eventually scrapped. (Author's Collection)

11

EXTENDED SERVICE

When they had carried their last passengers for their original operators, a number of buses were spared the prospect of being sold to another owner or even worse the dealer/breaker, or at least their fate was delayed, in some cases by years. These were the 'chosen few' who were retained to be deployed in other roles by the companies – the most obvious being the Driver Training Vehicle.

Normally painted out of the operator's standard livery, a variety of uses were found for these old omnibuses, from recovery vehicle to mobile canteen. The images in this chapter are but a small selection, but hopefully show the range of non-PSV tasks undertaken by withdrawn buses. It is pleasing to note that the importance of such buses in the fleets of yesteryear, and indeed more modern times, has been reflected in the number of ancillary vehicles which preservationists have rescued and restored to their latter-day condition.

New in 1958 to Trent Motor Services (1054), this Leyland PD3/4 had a high-capacity Willowbrook H41/32RD body. Initially the bus worked as a driver-trainer in normal fleet livery, but was then painted all-over white and carried both the Trent and National Bus Company decals. Note the folding-leaf doors on this fine double-decker which has been preserved by the company. (Photobus)

Bristol Omnibus L8468 was an LD6B from 1958, and is seen at the age of twenty-one in its new role, carrying all-over blue livery and large 'Driver Training Vehicle' signage. (Author's Collection)

Serving a dual purpose even in later life is ex-United Counties 964. Note not only is the 1954 Bristol KSW6B a learners' bus, but it is also used as a mobile recruitment centre for more drivers. This double-decker has since been restored to full company livery (above right) by the members of the Chelveston Preservation Group, started by ex-employees of UCOC, and who now own a whole range of Bristol vehicles from ex-Tilling Group companies. (Author's Collection/David J. Hancock)

The cutting-back of overhanging branches on trees along bus routes used to be the responsibility of the transport operator (is it ever thus?). Buses, mainly open-toppers, were designated tree-loppers. For obvious reasons, a lot of this safety work was done on Sundays, when crews would 'trim' off the offending foliage, and an open lorry would follow to collect the debris. Some companies had caged trailers towed by the bus itself, and the branches were thrown in there as they went along. *Above*: From the fleet of a long-gone, but fondly remembered independent operator comes this Guy Arab I with Brush bodywork. One of a trio delivered new to King Alfred Motor Services in 1942, the bus was withdrawn from service in 1951, and almost a decade later was still working for the company as a tree-lopper. (Author's Collection) *Below*: East Yorkshire Motor Services have been running bus services for over eighty years, and is still very much to the fore with a 300-strong fleet in the new millennium. From a bygone era, this Park-Royal Bridgemaster was new in 1961. Sixteen years later the double-decker, originally registered 4710 AT, came off normal duties, and was then sold off in 1985. (East Yorkshire Motor Services)

A 1950 Leyland PD2 with Bruce H30/26R, Newport Corporation No.31 was later deployed as a mobile cash office-cum-crew restroom. It is shown here in the Welsh city's bus stance in 1969. (Mike Street)

The crateful of milk bottles indicates that this ex-United Automobile Services double-decker has been downgraded to a mobile canteen/restroom. The location is Newcastle-upon-Tyne, near the riverside, as denoted by the Prudhoe Street Mission, a place of worship which still exists in some form. (Author's Collection)

A Tiger which has not lost its roar at more than seventy years of age! VR 5742 is a Leyland TS2 new in 1930 to Manchester Corporation. The thirty-two-seat body was built locally by Vulcan, but finished off by MCT. Surprisingly withdrawn from service after only nine years, the bus became 'A 87', an employees canteen, and is pictured here in the late 1950s / early '60s in that role, complete with what appears to be a roof-mounted water tank! The single-decker has been fully restored and housed in the excellent Manchester Museum of Transport (right). (R.F. Mack/D.G. MacDonald)

AEC Regent MXX 244 started life as bus RLH 44 in the London Transport fleet. In 1971 it was extensively rebuilt as service vehicle 581J, a mobile uniform issue unit for use by London Country. The Weymann-bodied vehicle, new in 1952, finally ended its working days in 1983, and has been in preservation since then. (Author's Collection)

Opposite page: Recovery vehicles and breakdown tenders are a necessary support in any operator's fleet. Many made neat conversions of withdrawn service buses to adapt to this purpose. *Above:* One of a pair of Roe-bodied Leyland PD3/4s delivered new to T. Severn & Sons of Dunscroft (Doncaster), 518 WY passed into South Yorkshire PTE ownership as a withdrawn vehicle when the independent was taken over. The vehicle then served well as a tow truck and was preserved in that condition, but in the latter SYT livery, and re-registered to OWJ 353A (inset). (Both Author's Collection) *Below:* 428 UFM began life at Chester in 1961 as a thirty-nine-seat coach with Crossville Motor Services (CMG 408). The Bristol MW was downgraded to bus-seating ten years later, and in 1978 converted to a recovery vehicle, based at Aberystwyth depot. The vehicle was transferred to North Western in late 1994 to continue in the same role. (Author's Collection)

This former Douglas Corporation (No.28) bus had a somewhat ignominious retirement. Withdrawn in 1963 at the age of twenty-eight, the AEC Regent (46 MAN) was sold to the Corporation's Water Department and converted into mobile Ladies Toilets for use at various outdoor events (such as the TT races). The Northern Counties-bodied vehicle was relieved of public (convenience) duties in 1971. By the spring of 1977 the bus had moved away from the Isle of Man, taken by the London Bus Preservation Group, based at Cobham. The AEC was sold to a Mr Bailey of Mansfield in the winter of 1984 for preservation, but after this date the vehicle history is unknown and it may have been scrapped (Author's Collection)

This is GRR 879, an AEC Regal 1 with Duple 'D-type' DP35F, new to Ebor Bus Co. (Mansfield, Notts) in 1946 as No.20. Ebor sold out to Mansfield District in 1950 and the Regal became No.33. Withdrawn during 1955, the single-decker became a snowplough for Midland General and Mansfield District. In those days every bus company had its own plough so that they could keep buses running when it snowed (more often then than they seem to nowadays!). (Author's Collection)

12

PEOPLE CARRIERS

Builders and contractors were not the only employers to provide staff transport. A diverse range of companies across mainly the manufacturing sector, many of whom had large workforces, decided it would be beneficial to 'bus-in' their key asset. Employees may have come from a wide catchment area, or factories were in out-of-town/remote sites and industrial estates, and it appeared to make economic sense to lay on free, or in some instances subsidised, transport to convey men and women to their places of work.

As in the construction industry, some firms hired from local bus or coach operators, but most made the ultimate decision to have their own vehicles to provide this service. In the twenty-first century, car ownership has made this practice all but redundant, and for businesses which do still require staff transport, hired or chartered vehicles are the order of the day.

In casting the net as wide as possible, the buses and coaches featured in this section represent but a few of the dozens of companies, many of whom no longer trade, who turned to second-hand omnibuses.

Above: Pictured a long way from its original operating territory, DHG 47 was part of a small fleet of buses used by Highlands Fabricators at Nigg on the Cromarty Firth in the north-west of Scotland. The company specialised in the construction of oil platforms, and is now part of the Barmac operation. The destination doesn't refer to Charles Dickens' famous residence at Broadstairs in Kent: the 'Bleak House' on the blind is a residential area of Burnley in Lancashire. *Above*: This all-Leyland PS2 was new in 1955 to Burnley, Colne and Nelson as No.47. (Author's Collection)

One of the iconic names in toy cars is surely 'Matchbox'. The brainchild of Lesney Products, which had been founded in 1947 by Leslie and Rodney Smith (no relation, just old school friends), the '1–75' range of pocket-sized diecast models brought playtime pleasure to generations of youngsters. From small premises, including an old pub, the company took over a factory at Barret's Grove in North London, before real expansion in 1967/68 to a new purpose-built centre at Edmonton, Essex and in 1969 to a factory vacated by Ekco Electronics Works on the Sweynes Industrial Estate at Rochford. With a

substantial workforce, staff transport was a virtual necessity, and the company built up its own fleet of vehicles, originally painted dark blue with 'Matchbox Toys' or 'Lesney Products' decals, and then a revised livery of white with coloured stripes and the revamped 'Matchbox' legend. Not surprisingly, Lesney initially deployed former London Transport cast-offs, especially RTs, and some served well for years. Parked up at Hackney in May 1978 is ex-RT 807. The Park Royal-bodied AEC was thirty years old, and had been one of the RTs with roof box route numbers. (Author's Collection)

Founded in 1956 by tycoon Sir Charles Clove, the British Shoe Corporation brought together famous High Street names like Saxone and Freeman Hardy Willis. The main factory was at Leicester with a huge workforce who had their own social and cricket clubs, and a fleet of blue-painted buses for staff transport. The mass influx of cheaper, imported footwear led to the BSC's demise. In the latter years of operation, BSC 'Shuttle' bus ETO 183L was an ex-Nottingham Fleetline, with characteristic Willowbrook H47/30D bodywork.

Only seventy-six Regent Low Height (RLH) double-deckers were built for London Transport, all with Weymann bodies, between 1950–52, and deployed on 'Country' green-livery service. KYY 510 (RLH10) was part of the first batch in 1950, and gave almost sixteen years' service. Dealer Dagenham Motors then sold the bus on to Elkes Biscuits of Uttoxeter, and the AEC is seen here in 1969 in the yard of Green Bus at Rugeley. Started as a small family business by Charles Henry Elkes, the company is still thriving, now part of the Fox's/Northern Foods empire, producing mainly 'own label' products for supermarket chains from its Dove Valley Bakeries where around 1,400 people are employed. (Dale Tringham)

Opposite above: Trundling down Manchester's Piccadilly in March 1965 is ex-Crossville SLA 49, originally KB49, carrying employees of the city's Waterworks Department. New in 1947, the Bristol L6A ended stage-carriage service at the age of fourteen. (Author's Collection)

Opposite below: A Leyland which stayed in its own 'backyard' for non-PSV use. The Leyland Olympian was one of a batch of six delivered new to John Fishwick of Leyland (No.28). After withdrawal, the Weymann-bodied bus went 'up the road' to the Leyland Paint & Wallpaper Co. as staff transport in this 'rainbow stripes' and white colour scheme (vinyl silk or non-drip gloss?). Ironically, the manufacturer, especially well known as a producer of coatings for the trade, moved their operation in the 1980s to Birstall in West Yorkshire! (Author's Collection)

Home-textiles company Chortex have been producing towels at their Victoria Mills in Horwich, Bolton for more than a century. To bring in workers from surrounding areas, ex-Southern National (1682) was used. The Bristol LS5G is shown outside the factory in the summer of 1975, with a 'sister' vehicle parked behind. (Author's Collection)

Opposite above: Poultry processors Buxted Chickens had an operation based at Dalton, North Yorkshire. 'Laying over' in nearby Thirsk is the company's RHN 69, a former Darlington Corporation Guy Arab. (Author's Collection)

Opposite below: The Brains sausage and meat pie factory at New Cheltenham, on the edge of Bristol, ran a fleet of ex-Bristol Omnibus Co. vehicles as staff buses, bought via dealers. On the early evening 'home' run in the autumn of 1976 is the former Bristol Omnibus Co. No.C3440, a Bristol-engined Bristol K-type new in 1949. It had completed its last fare-paying trip in 1965. (S. Dowle)

Above: Former Ribble Motor Services ACK 777 was a wartime Daimler with Brush 'Utility' body, which later went on to provide staff transport for Airtech Ltd. Second-hand buses were also used to transport customers! Enjoying a renaissance in the new millennium, bingo reached its original peak of popularity in the 1970s. In an age before supermarket giants laid on free bus services for shoppers, some bingo owners made it easier for their paying patrons to get to the 'housey-housey' by laying on transport from the suburbs and schemes of the towns and cities in which they ran the game of chance. One of the 'pioneers' of providing transport for Bingo-ers in Scotland was Bingorama/Top Flight Leisure of Lanarkshire, who had halls in Bellshill and Burnbank (Hamilton). With a fleet strength of around fifteen vehicles, latterly in the company's own 'Kingfisher' blue, but initially in the original owners' livery, the yard housed an eclectic mix of vehicle marques until they 'standardised' on Bristols and ultimately Leyland Atlanteans. *Below*: Parked up side-by-side in the mid-'70s is a pair of Leyland Titan PDs. On the left is JTD 383, a PD2/1 new to Lytham St Annes (No.12) with East Lancs rear-entrance body. THE 187 was still in 'Tracky' – Yorkshire Traction – colours. The double-decker had Northern Counties H35/28F bodywork and was new as No.1187 in 1960. (Both Author's Collection)

13

OVERSEAS OMNIBUSES

While people have left British shores to find new and better lives in foreign lands for centuries, the migration of buses to new owners across the continents, especially North America, is a far more recent practice! Starting in the 1960s, the 'trailblazer' was Omnibus Promotions, founded by English teacher Robert Thomas based in Boston, Mass. Having taken US school kids to the UK on sightseeing vacations and used a couple of ex-London Transport vehicles as part of his 'British Promotions' enterprise, he had the idea of reversing the trend and 'Omprom' was born, based in London. Others have followed, including Ensign and the London Bus Export Co.

Although dozens of former LT buses have made Atlantic crossings, so have others, especially ex-NBC/Tilling Bristol Lodekkas, although many ended up as big red 'London' buses to suit the US market. Former British buses can also be found closer to home in Europe. The pictures chosen for this section aim to show a cross-section of emigrant omnibuses, in various guises and countries!

Operating in six continents, Gray Line is one of the world's foremost sightseeing tour companies. In their Canadian/North American fleet is ex-LT RM1943. New in 1964 as ALD943B, the Routemaster was shipped to Canada in 1986. The double-decker initially worked for Piccadilly Tours in Ottawa and then Absolute Charters in Halifax, Nova Scotia, but had always retained its red livery. (Author's Collection)

Opposite page: Three-in-one to show the long life of this old omnibus! JRX 817 was originally Thames Valley 742, a Bristol KSW6B with ECW L53RD body, new in 1955, and shown with coach seating in Victoria Coach Station, London in the 1960s (centre). By the following decade, the bus had 'crossed the pond' and is captured (bottom) at the British Army's training unit at Suffield, Alberta, Canada during a 1975 world tour, still in Thames Valley livery. The top image features the Bristol almost thirty years later at a roadside antiques barn on Highway 33 in rural Ontario, Canada. (Author's Collection)

From the South of England to an idyllic island – a good move for this former Hants & Dorset FLF.
Withdrawn in the early 1980s, the Bristol enjoyed 'missionary' work with Newcourt Church in
London. Then followed a few years spent parked up with two dealers – Omnibus Promotions and
North's at Sherburn. By the end of 1994, the double-decker was in Hawaii, eventually fitted with
a Cummins engine and offside front entrance. After being red for the 'Sugar Cane Train' in Maui,
the bus was painted blue for tourist shuttle work between Kaanapali and historic Lahaina, the
largest town in West Maui. (Author's Collection)

Working in Belgium, but still displaying a Welsh blind, is UWO 688. The bus started life in 1958 as West Monmouthshire No.13, a PD2/38 with Willowbrook B31F body (above). In the summer of 1966 it was fitted with a Massey L27/28RD body (no.2680). (Top Author's Collection/Above John Kaye)

The fare from Amsterdam to Moscow would be costly! This ex-Potteries Motor Traction (PMT) (No.H701) is pictured in the Dutch city in Sundecker colours, a Channel Islands-based travel company. New in 1957 with Metro-Cammell H37/31F body, the bus was brought back to the UK in a sorry state and was seen as a long-term restoration project by new owners Quantock Heritage in Taunton. (Author's Collection)

Opposite above: This Scottish-built bus went to a land 'Down Under'! The Daimler Fleetline with contemporary Alexander 'AL' bodywork was new as WHL 274J, a Daimler CRG6LXB 'Fleetline', and delivered in May 1971 to West Riding as their No.274. The double-decker is seen here working as a City Sightseeing bus in Melbourne. (Author's Collection)

Opposite below: A former Mansfield & District FLF with a long and well-travelled history. New in 1867 as No.689, it became 489 in the East Midland Motor Services fleet in 1976. Withdrawn four years later, the Bristol bus had two other UK owners before Omnibus Promotions shipped her to Pennsylvania Tours in late 1985. Around five years on, the bus moved to Iowa City, bought by the Wig & Pen Restaurant, and was then bought by Dubuqueland Tours in the same US state. In the winter of 2000, the thirty-three-year-old double-decker was shipped to Japan from Los Angeles, and is seen here as a visitor bus for the Hida-Takayama Museum of Art. The offside entrance for American use had been removed, and the oriental owners had stated an intention to restore the bus to original condition. (Author's Collection)

To conclude the continental connections, two unknown British buses on foreign soil. *Above*: Parked up in Belgrade, Serbia as late as 2006 is this Bristol LD model. *Below*: In a Brussels side street stands the quintessential London bus, but the RT shows no signs of its original LT roots ... or should that be routes! (Both Author's Collection)

14

FAIRS' STAGE

When I was a boy in the 1960s, 'All the fun of the fair' extended beyond the dodgems, waltzers and other traditional rides. I was always intrigued, and admittedly sometimes intimidated by the sights and sounds of the array of vehicles on the peripheries of the site, in the shape of the showmen's lorries and especially the old buses. These withdrawn PSVs were an integral part of 'the shows' for several decades, as living accommodation, generators, equipment carriers, or a mixture of all three!

Dating back as early as the 1930s, the fairground owners of the United Kingdom (and later in some parts of Europe, especially France) turned to cast-off omnibuses as an economical method of acquiring ancillary vehicles. An accepted consensus of opinion as to the origins of this practice concurs that the provision of more electricity and the means to generate the power, provided in earlier days by traction engines, became an absolute necessity on the modern fairground. The showmen bought petrol-electric vehicles sold out-of-service by Tilling Stevens, and the trend soon grew among the fairground fraternity. Up until the end of the 1960s, and in a few cases into the opening years of the following decade, ageing buses and coaches were a common sight in the travelling fair, some even still wearing the livery of their previous operators.

VT 846 was a BMMO 'SOS QL' new in August 1928 with a Brush B37F body to Potteries Motor Traction as No.147, one of a batch of fifty delivered that year. (Author's Collection)

Opposite above & below: Founded at Maidstone in 1897 as W.A. Stevens, a petrol-electric vehicle had been offered in 1906. A key customer, Thomas Tilling, who had many omnibus interests, took over the company and it became Tilling-Stevens, chiefly to produce petrol-electric bus chassis. Here are two fine examples of Tilling-Stevens vehicles being snapped up for fairground use. *Above*: WW 7102 was new in 1929 to Bristol Tramways & Carriage Co., who were taken over by the Tilling group two years later. (Author's Collection) *Below*: New in 1938 to Stratford-upon-Avon Blue Motors Ltd (Stratford Blue), this T.S. B10A2 with thirty-two-seat body gave ten years' service as fleet No.16 before being bought by a showman, in whose ownership it is seen in the 1950s. (R.H.G. Simpson)

An Albion with a real nomadic life was VA 8675. New to Stewart & MacDonald in 1929, the bus joined the Central SMT ranks as A5 upon takeover three years later. Passing across the county to firstly Gorman of Coatbridge and then Baxter's of Airdrie, the PMA28 was acquired by E. Sedgwick of Salford around 1940, and was last licensed in 1956. (A.E. Jones)

While single-deck vehicles were in the majority on the fairgrounds, some showmen did buy double-deckers. Still in its former owner's livery and showing fleet No. 333, this 1948 all-Leyland PD1A with H30/26R bodywork was new to Salford Corporation, and gave fifteen years' service to the municipal operator. (Author's Collection)

Opposite above: The origins of this Leyland TS8 are clearly evident in this shot. The vehicle was new in 1939 to Alexander as P566, with the fleet plate visible on the bonnet panel which is propped against the nearside wheel. It also appears the thirty-five-coach-seated single-deck still wears the famous blue livery, with the cream flash. The vehicle was bought out-of-service by a Kilmarnock showman. (Author's Collection)

Opposite below: JNW 376 was a 1940 Leylan Tiger TS8, new to Wallace Arnold. Its original Duple body was replaced by this Burlingham body twelve years later. Withdrawn in 1954, the coach passed to N. O'Hara of Spennymoor, and the following year was on loan to Wilkinson in Darlington. As shown here in this view from *c.*1960, the Leyland was later acquired by a showman. (Author's Collection)

Double-deckers were often cut down to size by their fairground owners, to suit their new role. GLF 665 was a wartime utility-bodied Guy Arab Mark 1 delivered new to London Transport in 1942 as G15. (Author's Collection)

Opposite above: AHN 367 was a Bristol GO5G dating from 1934. The 'chopped' double-decker is seen on the shows circuit over twenty years later. (R.F. Mack)

Opposite below: This Guy Arab started life with Durham Services, and remained in the North East after withdrawal. (Author's Collection)

BJA 441 entered service with North Western Road Car in 1947 as their No.141. Upon withdrawal eleven years later, the Bristol L5G passed to a Nottingham contractor via Frank Cowley, the Salford dealer. By the summer of 1961, the thirty-five-seat ECW-bodied bus had been acquired by a showman from Haydock, Liverpool. It is caught on camera at the Hazel Grove Agricultural Show in Stockport in July 1965. When the Bristol's fairground days were over, it ended up being used as a shed for many years in Salford, where the body basically rotted and fell off and was beyond repair. In 2006, William Stainforth from Stroud rescued the vehicle to restore the chassis/cab as a demonstration chassis. (Author's Collection)

Opposite above: The 'TMT' legend shows this BMMO SOS was in the fleet of Trent Motor Traction, new in 1939 as No.643, with Willowbrook C31F body. (Author's Collection)

Opposite below: UF 7410 was a Leyland Titan TD1 / Short Brothers H50R bus (with a sliding roof!), new in 1931 as Southdown No.910. It was withdrawn early in 1939 and went to Wilts & Dorset in the June as their No.23. This was one of eighty-five double-deckers brought into the W&D fleet from various sources to cope with wartime troop and worker movements around the Salisbury Plain area. It was given a new ECW fifty-two-seat low-bridge body in September 1941, and remained in service until April 1953 when it was bought by a Mr Stanley (showman) of Watford. It was still recorded as being with him as late as August 1960. (Author's Collection)

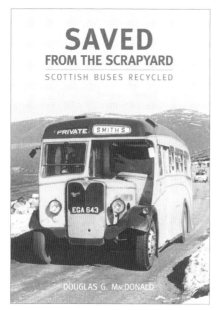

Saved from the Scrapyard:
Scottish Buses Recycled
DOUGLAS MACDONALD

What happens to a bus when it reaches the end of its life? Most people would visualise a rusting frame residing in a scrapyard, waiting to be broken up. However, many buses are rescued from this fate, and enjoy long, varied, and fruitful lives after their retirement from passenger duties. In his inimitable and humorous style, Douglas MacDonald looks at the changing bus scene in Scotland since the 1950s and the fascinating range of different tasks undertaken by the country's old buses. The ageing vehicles have been used as polling booths, showmen's transport, recovery trucks, car transporters, mobile canteens, mobile homes, and much more. With over 200 photographs, accompanied by intriguing facts and anecdotes, *Saved From the Scrapyard* explores the afterlife of the rescued Scottish bus.

978 0 7524 3880 1

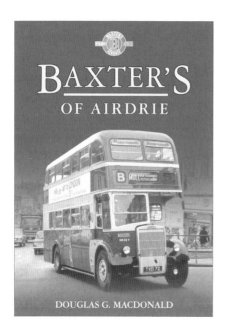

Baxter's of Airdrie
DOUGLAS MACDONALD

Baxter's is an Airdrie institution. The family-owned bus company has been in existence well over half a century and its blue buses a regular sight in the Monklands area. There can be no one living in the North Lanarkshire area who has not travelled on one of their buses. Douglas MacDonald, a life-long bus enthusiast, tells the story in words and pictures of this Lanarkshire enterprise.

978 0 7524 4229 7

City to the Black Country:
A Nostalgic Journey by Bus & Tram
DAVID HARVEY

This fascinating collection of archive photographs takes the reader on a nostalgic bus and tram ride through the north-west of Birmingham, from the city centre along the A41 to Hockley, taking in the famous Jewellery Quarter and the many Victorian housing developments around Handsworth. Travelling through numerous shopping centres and the important town centre of West Bromwich with its 'golden mile', the route splits at Carter's Green. This entertaining book is sure to delight local residents and transport enthusiasts alike.

978 0 7524 5297 5

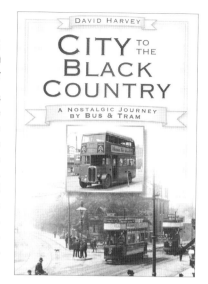

Luton Corporation Transport
PETER ROSE

This book covers the history of municipal transport in Luton from the first horse-drawn buses and the town's electric trams, through to the sale of the undertaking in 1970 to United Counties, the bus company which dominated services in the rest of Bedfordshire. Fully illustrated, and including comprehensive information on the buses operated by Luton Corporation Transport and the routes they served, this book will have a nostalgic appeal to all who have lived and worked in Luton during the Corporation era as well as many bus enthusiasts nationwide.

978 0 7524 4913 5

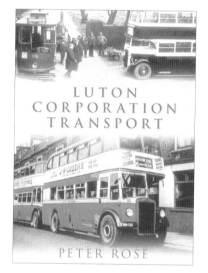

The London Bus Story
JOHN CHRISTOPHER

The archetypal Routemaster is arguably the most recognised vehicle in the world. Buses have been operating on London's streets since 1829, originally with horse-drawn omnibuses, with the first motorised buses making an appearance in 1902. For six decades London went its own way with specially designed buses, although the 'bendy' bus has not proved popular, yet even today the London bus holds a nostalgic and much-loved position in our hearts.

978 0 7524 5084 1

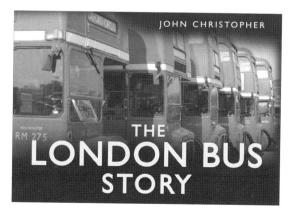

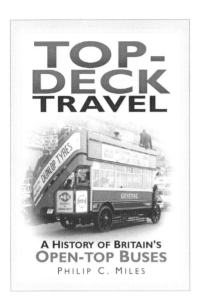

Top-deck Travel:
A History of Open-top Buses
PHILIP C. MILES

This illustrated history charts the development of the open-top bus, from the early 1900s when buses ordinarily had an open top-deck to the bustling sightseeing operations so popular around the world today, recalling many operators along the way who have since been relegated to the annals of history. Following trends around the UK, from London and the south coast to the north and Scotland, author and enthusiast Philip C. Miles has collated many unusual descriptions and photographs showing these buses at work.

978 0 7524 5137 4

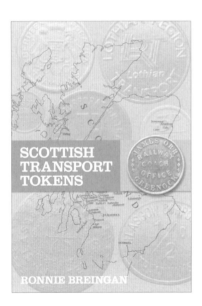

Scottish Transport Tokens
RONNIE BREINGAN

Most transport tokens in Scotland were introduced in the middle of the nineteenth century, but until recent years they did not attract many collectors. The collecting and study of tokens has now become a branch of numismatics. The early tokens were usually struck in brass, copper or bronze, but as we moved into the twentieth century celluloid ones were introduced, followed by plastics and fibres as well as metals. Tokens were in fact the tickets of their time. Paper tickets did not come into use until about the 1880s and in Glasgow on the tramways from the late 1870s. By selling a number of tokens transport firms were assured of the custom of these passengers as well as the security of the conductor. This fascinating book reveals the history of tokens in Scotland.

978 0 7524 4764 3

Visit our website and discover thousands of other History Press books.
www.thehistorypress.co.uk